JL

Know About Abuse

KNOW
ABOUT
ABUSE

Margaret O. Hyde

Walker and Company   New York

First published in the United States of America in 1992
by Walker Publishing Company, Inc.

Published simultaneously in Canada by Thomas Allen & Son
Canada, Limited, Markham, Ontario

Library of Congress Cataloging-in-Publication Data
Hyde, Margaret O. (Margaret Oldroyd)
    Know about abuse / Margaret O. Hyde.
        p.   cm.
    Summary: Describes cases of emotional, physical, and sexual abuse;
their effects; and how to prevent maltreatment.
    Includes index.
    ISBN 0-8027-8176-4 —ISBN 0-8027-8177-2 (reinf.)
    1. Child abuse—United States—Juvenile literature.   [1. Child
abuse.]   I. Title.
HV6626.5.H94   1992
362.7'6—dc20   92-2822
                                                          CIP
                                                          AC

Photograph on p. 38, © Wolf Baschung,
appears courtesy of Hale House Center

Printed in the United States of America

10 9 8 7 6 5 4 3 2 1

Contents

Acknowledgments   vii

1. Broken Bones and Nasty Words:
   Yesterday and Today   1

2. Abuse at Any Age   13

3. Battered by Drugs Before Birth   25

4. Abused and Homeless   41

5. Children of Battered Women   53

6. Sexual Abuse   63

7. What Can You Do?   73

Where to Find Help   83

Glossary   85

For Further Reading   89

Index   91

Acknowledgments

The author wishes to thank the many abused children and adults abused as children who have contributed to this book. Statistics and other information from the American Medical Association, Child Help USA, The National Coalition Against Domestic Violence, The National Committee for the Prevention of Child Abuse, and The U.S. Advisory Board on Child Abuse and Neglect have been especially helpful. Photographs from the Northern Westchester Shelter for Victims of Domestic Violence were greatly appreciated.

Know About Abuse

1.

Broken Bones and Nasty Words:
Yesterday and Today

"**F**ather charged with hiding son in closet for years." "Mother accused of drowning baby." "Son abuses elderly mother." "Battered wife charged with killing husband." Although some of today's family violence makes the headlines, much of it is as hidden as it was in the days before recorded history. Even though efforts are being made to help the victims in today's world who suffer from broken bones, nasty words, and other kinds of abuse, an alarming amount of abuse continues to occur.

Most abusers and their victims do not stand out from the crowd. Abuse occurs in all kinds of families, no matter where they live, how much money they have, or what their skin color is. Your neighbor, a friend at school, the person who delivers your paper, a teacher you know, or just about anyone may be a victim of abuse. Most of the victims hide the hurt. Too few know how to reach out for the help that can change their lives and make them better.

Abuse takes many forms, such as severe physical

3

punishment or other hurts to the body, forced sexual contact, neglect, and invisible hurts such as threats and put-downs. Being disciplined in ways that leave scars or bruises, being hurt for no special reason, being made to feel like a nobody, being touched in a way that makes you uncomfortable, and being tricked or coaxed into sexual acts are just some of the ways children and young adults are abused.

Understanding and awareness help to prevent abuse. This means looking behind the headlines. Consider the case of Jean, whose baby nearly died from neglect. The newspaper article about a mother whose toddler was severely burned was small, and most people who read it probably forgot about it almost at once. A few may have wondered, What kind of mother could this person be?

This mother, Jean, was fifteen when her step-father raped her. He left home when he found out she was pregnant. Their son, Tommy, was born the following summer. Jean tried going back to school, but she could not manage living with her mother. In less than a month, she quit school and found a one-room apartment. She lived on her welfare check.

At first, Jean hoped the baby would love her and fill the empty feeling that she had inside. But the baby cried a great deal, and Jean was sure he would not cry so much if he really loved her. She struggled to make a home for him for two long years. Even though Jean loved her son, there were many days when she thought about leaving him in the park so some nice person would take him home and care for him.

Jean felt more like a teen than a single mother. After all, she had not asked for the baby. She felt she still had a right to go to parties with her friends. She decided to take Tommy to the next party with her and let him sleep in her friend's bedroom while she partied downstairs.

By midnight, a very drunken Jean managed to get to her own apartment and put Tommy in his room. He screamed when she tried to put him in bed, so she let him play on the floor while she ran the water in the bathtub. Before Jean turned off the hot water, she passed out on her bed. The next thing she remembered was the sound of knocking on the door.

Water from the tub had run through the ceiling into the apartment below. Jean's neighbor had tried to reach her by phone, but she did not answer. When he called 911, the police who came found Tommy lying on the bathroom floor in scalding hot water. Quick work on the part of the police saved his life, but he was severely burned. Jean was charged with neglect, taken to a detention center, and released into a program that would help her learn better parenting. Tommy was placed in foster care when he left the hospital. At some time in the future, he may be returned to his mother.

This is just one of the many cases of child abuse and neglect that make the newspapers. Although many cases do not, abandonment is one kind that is often noted. In ancient times, abandonment was so common that it was not unusual to find the bodies of babies in rivers, dung heaps, cesspools, and latrines.

Abandonment was still common in Europe in the eighteenth century, when about one in three children was left with no care or given to others. Many parents gave their children away. Some left them where they would be found, because the family was too poor to feed them or was ashamed of a child's physical or mental handicap. Some simply hoped rich people would find the baby and give him or her a better life than the family could provide.

Through the years, neighbors and relatives believed that whatever happened behind the closed doors of a family's home was none of anybody's business. Many still feel that way, but society has come a long way from the days in which parents tried to "beat the devil" out of their children, believing it was their righteous duty to break children of their evil impulses. Many teachers, religious leaders, and parents still believe the old

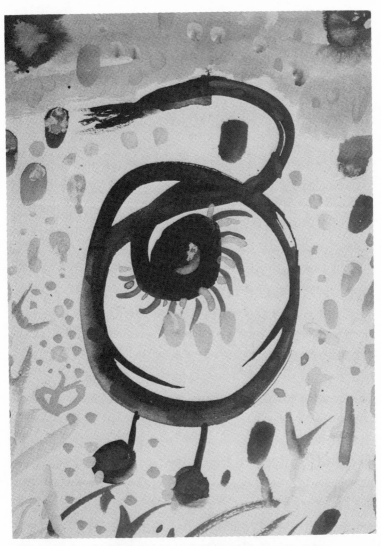

THE ABUSED GIRL WHO DREW THIS PICTURE DESCRIBED HER DRAWING AS A FIRE-EATING SNAKE ABOUT TO HIT SOMEONE. SHE SAID THAT THE EYE REPRESENTS HERSELF. DOCTORS SUGGEST THAT SHE WAS EXPRESSING A FEELING OF BEING TRAPPED IN HER FAMILY SITUATION.

saying "Spare the rod and spoil the child." Although most spankings were probably not severe, many children were taken to doctors with serious injuries by parents who said they "fell down the stairs." And many more were allowed to heal or die without medical help.

Old records of mothers beating their babies to stop them from screaming show their good intent. For example, one mother wrote to her friend that she whipped her son until he was black and blue, and until she could not whip him anymore. "He never gave up one single inch," she wrote. This mother planned to teach her child a lesson by beating him again until he got over his screaming. Her son was three and a half months old. About a hundred years ago, this woman was considered an outstanding member of the community, and her child-rearing methods were quite acceptable.

The first public defense of a beaten child did not come until 1874, after an investigation of a report that a child in New York City was chained to her bed and beaten by her adoptive parents. At that time, there was no child protection agency, but the Society for the Prevention of Cruelty to Animals came to her rescue by pointing out that she was a member of the animal kingdom.

Dr. C. Henry Kempe and his colleagues introduced the term *battered child syndrome* in 1962, after checking with other hospitals to see if they too had many cases in which the symptoms of the children did not seem to fit the explanations given by the parents. This famous pioneer in the field of child abuse noted that many babies and toddlers under the age of three were brought to the hospital by parents who said they fell down the steps, upset hot water, were hit on the head with a brother's toys, fell out of the crib, and so on. Examinations of many children revealed broken bones that had already healed and other evidence of earlier injuries.

By 1974, about 60,000 cases of child abuse were reported in the United States. In 1980 the number rose to one million. By 1990 about 2.5 million cases of child abuse and neglect were reported. Although some of these cases were not proven, as many as 50% of cases were probably never even reported.

The increase in the number of reports of child maltreatment has been called astronomical. Although some of the increase may be the result of better awareness, experts believe that there has also been a real increase in the amount of abuse. One recent report describes the amount of child abuse and neglect in the United States today as a national emergency.

Although not all cases of abuse are tragic and serious, thousands of children are being starved, abandoned, burned, severely beaten, berated and belittled, and sexually abused each year. Imagine a seventeen-year-old who has spent his entire life in a cellar, or a child who fills the role of parent to her seven brothers and sisters while her mother is drunk. Consider the case of a twelve-year-old whose newborn baby was wrapped in a garbage bag and dropped into a trash bin, where he was rescued by someone who heard his cry. Or the case of a five-year-old girl who died from a broken neck in a room where her nine-year-old brother was found huddled in a closet. Many of his bones were broken.

There are a great many tragic cases of abuse, and each one is different. The majority of abused children never make the headlines, but thousands of children die each year because of maltreatment. According to Childhelp USA, a national child abuse prevention program, a child is attacked by one or both parents every two minutes. Two to five children die and twelve suffer permanent brain damage from abuse each day.

Much abuse goes far beyond the physical abuse of beatings, bruises, and broken bones. Emotional abuse is much more common than most people realize. Often it takes the form of verbal battering. Lyn's mother tells her, "Get your ugly face out of my sight." Lyn, who is actually very attractive, sees what she thinks is an ugly face whenever she looks in the mirror. Remarks such as "You are stupid" can make a child believe that he or she *is* stupid. Emotional abusers say things like "Behave or I will leave you to take care of yourself," or "You are a slut, just like your mother."

Emotional battering hurts. It may do as much damage as physical abuse or more. As most people know, the old saying "Sticks and stones may break my bones, but words will never hurt me" is not really true at all.

One kind of abuser, who is seldom recognized, is an overly protective parent. For instance, a father who will not allow his eight-year-old daughter to play with other children in the neighborhood may be an abuser. He tells her they are not good enough for her, but he really wants to prevent her from making friends in an effort to keep all her affection for himself. This prevents her from developing normal friendships and is a form of emotional abuse.

Sexual abuse is so common that an estimated 25 to 35 percent of women and 10 to 20 percent of men in the United States were victims of sexual abuse as children. And many cases have probably remained secret. It is estimated that more than one in six Americans have been sexually abused. The effects of such abuse, described in Chapter 6, hurt everyone.

Although parents have come a long way in understanding their children since the days when babies were wrapped in swaddling clothes, the amount of physical, emotional, and sexual abuse and neglect that children experience is staggering.

2.

Abuse at Any Age

*B*abies look sweet when they smile and coo, but a baby presents a different picture to a mother who cannot sleep because her child screams all night. Many parents have said they have felt like beating their babies when they cried a lot, especially at night. But some mothers and fathers do more than feel like beating them—they do it.

One doctor reported the case of an eighteen-month-old boy who was brought to him with second- and third-degree burns on his legs and buttocks. One leg was burned from his foot to his knee, but the other leg was burned only a few inches above the ankle. His mother claimed that she had left the baby in the tub when she went to answer the phone and he had turned on the hot water. The doctor did not believe her. In such a case, both legs would have been burned to the same height. The doctor also noted that it takes a long time to raise the temperature of bathwater to the scalding point. Besides, the mother would have been alerted by the child's cries. He thought it likely that the mother had held the child and dangled his legs in scalding water.

Many parents who abuse babies are overwhelmed by stress, have never learned how to handle their feelings, or expect too much of their children. For many adults, beating is a means of staying in control and the main form of discipline. These parents do evil in order "to do good," so they feel no guilt. For example, many parents have burned the hands of their children, sometimes severely, believing that this would teach them not to play with matches. This kind of child rearing tends to pass from generation to generation.

A typical case of a parent who expects babies to learn from physical punishment is one in which a father beat his little boys, aged five months and eighteen months. When a neighbor reported the problem to a social worker, the boys were found to be suffering from multiple bruises, cuts, and fractures. Another parent, Holly T., said her five-and-a-half-month-old baby was lazy and stubborn, and thus needed discipline. A fractured skull and pelvis were the results of such discipline.

Many alarms have been sounded about abuse in nursery schools and day-care centers. Although it is the exception, the abuse of young children by people entrusted with their care does happen. Consider the case of Elvira, a three-year-old who goes to a day-care center while her parents work.

She seems happy to go "to school." It makes her feel important to go to school the way her older brothers and sisters do. But Elvira's school is different in a number of ways. Her brother Brian discovered one of them.

Each evening at dinnertime, when the family talked about their day, Brian noted that Elvira was unusually quiet. One evening, when asked what games she played, she mentioned the "butt game." Then she covered her mouth with her hands and said she couldn't tell them about it because it was a special secret.

When Brian was alone with Elvira that evening, he reminded her that she told him all her secrets. He asked her to tell him about the butt game. Elvira would only say that the teacher took pictures of the kids during the game, but she said she knew she would get in trouble if she told anyone about it. She begged Brian to keep her secret. If he didn't, she believed something awful might happen to her.

Brian was old enough to suspect that something was very wrong. He alerted his parents, who were able to uncover the whole story. In the butt game the teacher was taking pictures of nude children and later selling the photos to men who passed them along to sex magazines sold on the black market. Investigations took a long time, but it did not take long for Elvira's parents to know that they needed to spend more time talking with her. Elvira learned that people who ask children to keep secrets from their parents may be doing something wrong and that she was right in telling her brother about that kind of secret. It also did not take her parents long to find a different day-care center for her.

Many cases of sexual abuse in day-care centers and nursery schools have been coming to light in recent years, but this does not mean that these are risky places for children to be. More parents and school systems are screening teachers and requiring higher standards for places where young children are cared for outside their homes.

Older brothers and sisters are helping to check conditions through careful listening and discussion of what goes on during the day. Threats by abusers often cause behavior that makes family members suspicious. Physical symptoms, pain, fears, and sexual behavior are among the signs of scare tactics used by abusers who fear the children might tell.

The average age of abused children is about seven years old, but children can suffer from abuse at any age. Most of today's parents understand that babies cannot be expected to learn good behavior from beatings, but there are many who still batter their children from birth till adolescence with the intent of improving their behavior. Adolescents are able to hide their physical injury, and, like children,

THIS DRAWING BY AN ADOLESCENT WAS DESCRIBED AS A SELF-PORTRAIT. CHILD ABUSE CAN LEAD TO A LACK OF SELF-CONTROL AND SELF-ESTEEM. IN THIS CASE IT LED TO DRUG ABUSE AND FAILURE IN SCHOOL AND A TEENAGER WHO SAW HIMSELF AS LESS THAN A PERSON.

they often do so for fear of being removed from their homes or causing a parent to be sent to jail.

Some adolescents cover their hurt by becoming withdrawn. They have a hard time getting along with friends and teachers, and show little self-confidence in sports and everything they do. "There is nothing anybody will like about me" is a typical expression of the teen who feels like damaged goods.

Many teens in trouble become teens who make trouble. These abused adolescents feel the need to prove that friends, teachers, and parents still like them, so they do things that make others angry. This may even reach the point of serious misbehavior.

Thirteen-year-old Pam is such a person. She felt afraid and alone after her mother remarried. She hated the way her stepfather pawed her, and she swore at him to stop. When they argued, her mother blamed Pam and acted as if her straitlaced husband could do no wrong. She agreed with him when he suggested that Pam should be locked out of the house. Pam left, but she had no place to go. She thought her mother might believe her if she talked to her again, so Pam broke the window and climbed into her room. When her parents found her there, they punished her by cutting her hair very short. Pam could not let her friends see her this way, so she holed up in her room for weeks.

When Pam went back to school, she was sure her friends no longer liked her. She had always felt that there was something wrong with her anyhow. Maybe it was her fault that her mother and stepfather argued so much. She hated herself. How could anyone like her? She refused invitations from her old friends because she was sure they just felt sorry for her. She made new friends with a few kids who were always in trouble.

When her grades fell, Pam's favorite teacher talked to her about her problems and helped her to understand that much of what had happened at home was not really her fault. She helped Pam to see that her actions were really a cry for help. In this case, that cry was answered by an understanding teacher who helped to make Pam feel accepted in spite of her problems at home.

Many young people have no one who understands what is happening to them. Adolescence is not a peaceful time in the lives of any family members. It is a time of conflict for all young people because most are learning to relate to the opposite sex in a new way, becoming more independent, and beginning to work toward their careers. At the same time, many parents feel threatened by the growing independence of their children. Some *expect* trouble from teenagers, even though most young people grow up without causing any serious problems. Only the delinquents make the headlines.

When adolescents are abused, people tend to ask what they did to deserve the bad treatment. Abused adolescents are not as appealing as abused children, so there is less public sympathy for their plight. However, the abuse of teens is common. Studies suggest that as many as half the victims of abuse and neglect in the United States may be adolescents and that three quarters of the cases are never reported or referred to child protective agencies.

Battered women, like adolescents, are often blamed rather than being thought of as victims. Women are abused by their husbands, or boyfriends, at the rate of one every fifteen seconds. Two to four thousand women are beaten to death annually in the United States, and more than 50 percent of all married women will be assaulted at least once during their marriages. More than 35 percent of women will be repeatedly assaulted.

Even old people are not free from abuse. About 2.5 million elderly people live in terror in their own homes. Many are abused by their spouses, by adult children who are their caregivers, by grandchildren who live with them, by other relatives, or by those employed to care for them. The abused may be punched, have their Medicare money stolen, or even be murdered. Others may be hit with their own canes, deprived of adequate food, or left in dirty clothing that they are unable to change. The worst abusers of the elderly are adult children with alcohol and/or other drug problems.

Many abused elderly don't report their problems 3870/frmtthey will lose their shelter. They are afraid of being sent to a nursing home—where they think the abuse might be worse. Many blame themselves for not having been better parents.

Abuse of many kinds happens to people at any

age, from birth to death. Although society is beginning to be more aware of the amount of abuse, and to understand the need for prevention and help for the victims, much more needs to be done. You can play a part by learning more about abuse.

3.

Battered by Drugs Before Birth

An overwhelming number of babies suffer from drugs and diseases that affect them before they are born. Many of them are born to mothers who are not even aware that they are being abusive. Hospitals in many urban areas are reporting that 10 to 40 percent of their newborns have been exposed to drugs.

Loving, caring women can get involved with drugs without realizing how they can ruin their lives and those of their babies. Many of these women have been sexually abused and think they are no good, and/or live with families or in neighborhoods where substance abuse is very common.

Some addicts try very hard to stop using drugs while they are pregnant, but they are not always successful. Others believe the old myth that drugs cannot cross the placenta, an organ that develops on the uterus to feed the fetus, or unborn baby, by way of the umbilical cord. Many pregnant women do not care whether their drugs pass through the placenta. Some do not even know how to care.

Pregnant addicts need the attention of a doctor

even if they decide to stop or have stopped taking drugs. For instance, Jane is a heroin addict who knew that her baby would become addicted if she did not give up her drug use. She thought about stopping cold turkey, giving up all heroin use and suffering the withdrawal cramps, sweating, aching, and other symptoms. The description *cold turkey* comes from one of these symptoms—the goose-flesh look of skin during withdrawal. Before stopping her heroin use, Jane learned that her baby could die if she did not stop gradually. Her doctor gave her controlled amounts of a substitute drug, methadone. She and her baby would become addicted to it, but the amounts of methadone could be controlled. This would protect them from the impure and unknown strength of street drugs and be safer for both. Jane's newborn baby would still suffer and need special care, but it would not be in the same danger as it would from the kind of abuse that heroin would cause.

Heroin-addicted babies have been a recognized tragedy for many years, but other drugs also cause abuse to unborns. Crack, the inexpensive smokable form of cocaine, is at the root of physical and emotional problems for hundreds of thousands of babies today. Many other illegal drugs, such as marijuana, heroin, PCP, and LSD, can harm the unborn too. Pregnant addicts who inject illegal drugs also risk spreading AIDS and hepatitis B to

28

their babies through the use of unclean needles that carry these viruses.

Drugs that are legal for adults cause problems too. For example, the use of tobacco increases the chances of babies' being born early or being born dead.

Infants born to smokers are, on the average, about seven ounces lighter than babies of non-smokers and need more medical care after they are born. The babies of smokers have twice the risk of sudden infant death syndrome, also called crib death because these babies are found dead in their cribs for no obvious reason.

You may know someone who is trying to give up smoking with the help of a program called Because I Love My Baby from the American Lung Association. Or you may know girls or women who are making a decision to start or stop smoking. Even if they do not plan to have a baby soon, knowing that smoking is a form of drug abuse that can have serious effects on the fetus may help them to decide against starting.

Alcohol is a legal drug for adults, but it reaches the unborn when pregnant women drink. Many of these women have never heard of fetal alcohol syndrome (FAS), but it is one of the most common causes of mental retardation in the Western world.

Sixteen-year-old Doreen knows about fetal alcohol syndrome because her cousin, Hillary, has a son who was born with it. His head is unusually small, his face is flattened, there is a large space between his lips and his nose, and his eyelids droop. He also has problems sitting still, has mental retardation, does not hear or see well, and has seizures. Doreen blames Hillary for drinking too much before he was born. Their doctor agrees with her.

Doreen, who has just discovered she is pregnant, says she will be careful that her baby does not suffer from FAS. She knows that Hillary drank a lot of gin while she was pregnant, but she will only drink beer. Unfortunately, it does not matter what kind of alcohol she drinks. If Doreen drinks at all during her pregnancy, she is taking a risk.

When a pregnant woman drinks alcohol, it circulates in her blood and in the blood of her unborn child within minutes. Nurses have reported that they can smell alcohol during the delivery of a baby whose mother had been drinking.

Alcohol hurts the fetus much more than it hurts the mother, for the fetus is growing and changing at a rapid rate. Among other things, it may interfere with the amount of oxygen that reaches its brain, causing brain damage.

Avoiding alcohol is the only way to be sure that a baby will not be the victim of alcohol abuse before it even takes its first breath. No one knows how much alcohol is a safe amount for a pregnant woman to drink. It is known that there is no safe time to drink during pregnancy.

About 6 million American women are alcoholics or alcohol abusers. Certainly, alcoholic women are at the highest risk of bearing children with FAS. They suffer from a disease in which they crave alcohol and continue to use it even when it causes problems in their lives. Their thinking is distorted, so usually they deny that they have an alcohol problem. Even the knowledge that alcohol can cause many birth defects may mean little compared with their addiction to it.

If a pregnant woman stops drinking, she reduces the risk of FAS and of a less severe condition, known as fetal alcohol effect (FAE). An FAE child is likely to have fewer symptoms, but decreased birth weight, abnormal growth, and behavioral problems are still present in children with FAE.

Many children whose mothers drink are born without problems, but others, who seem normal at birth, show symptoms later in life. Unfortunately, when FAS is present, the problems do not decrease as the children grow older. Even FAE children may never be able to live independently.

Michael Dorris, in his book *The Broken Cord*, tells the heartbreaking story of his experiences with his adopted son Adam, whose Sioux Indian parents both died of alcohol abuse. The book includes descriptions of how Adam just closed the door when he saw water running all over the bathroom after a pipe broke, how he bought a doughnut for ten dollars and didn't ask for change, and how he didn't think to wear his coat on very cold days. Dorris's love for Adam shines through the book, along with his rage at the abuse Adam suffered because his mother drank before he was born.

Fetal alcohol syndrome cannot be cured, but it can be prevented. You can help to spread the word to friends about the importance of not drinking beer, wine, wine coolers, or any other alcoholic beverage if they are pregnant. Although many young people have some idea about the possible effect of alcohol on unborn children, many are not aware of how serious the problems can be.

Each year, FAS affects thousands of babies in the United States, and thousands more are born with FAE. Recent studies show that there has been an increase in the number of young women who are heavy drinkers. This may well mean there will be more children who suffer from drug abuse before they are born.

Tobacco and alcohol are often just two of the drugs used in combination by pregnant women. Another popular drug is marijuana. Pregnant women who smoke marijuana have an increased risk of having babies who are born early, are born dead, or have lower birth weights. Because pot is stored in fatty tissues, it tends to remain in the fetus. Scientists who study marijuana are blaming it for a variety of physical and behavioral problems in infants whose mothers used it while pregnant or passed it on to their babies in their breast milk.

Today cocaine is used by about a million women of childbearing age, and it is responsible for large numbers of addicted and impaired babies. The March of Dimes estimates that 2 to 4 million babies addicted to crack will be born by the year 2000. The tragedy of crack babies makes the headlines in newspapers across the nation. Some of these babies suffer from seizures, cerebral palsy, or mental retardation. Not all babies whose mothers used illegal drugs have such severe problems, but doctors say that even one "hit" of cocaine during pregnancy can cause lasting damage to the child. Although a single dose of cocaine and the chemicals it forms clear out of the mother's body within two days, the unborn baby is exposed for four days.

Tim is a two-year-old who has a pixieish smile, but sometimes he freezes in one position for minutes at a time. The smile stays on his face, but no one knows what he is thinking. Sometimes he just sits among a roomful of toys, not making any effort to play with them. Or he may throw the toys for reasons others do not understand.

The babies in the day-care center where Tim spends his days have all suffered from exposure to crack and other drugs before they were born. Some of them startle easily and are overwhelmed by even small amounts of stimulation. They are soothed by quiet touches, but a quick move toward them can cause a scream. These babies are given to spasms, trembling, and high-pitched whining that sounds like cat cries, and they may well be in pain that they cannot express except through long periods of crying. Many of them tend to arch their backs and become rigid when someone tries to cuddle them.

Buffy was adopted by parents who were told that her mother had used drugs when she was pregnant. She seemed to be fine except for a mild form of cerebral palsy. The new parents felt that they could overcome anything with their love for Buffy. But this did not prove to be true. They soon learned that she was overly sensitive to light, touch, and sound. She would bite and kick her mother when her diaper was changed, and she had no interest in the toys that please most babies. Sometimes her muscles grew rigid. Buffy did not babble and coo the way most babies do.

When Buffy grew older, she had difficulty talking and understanding. Her parents continue to love her, but they do not expect her to overcome all the abuse she received before she was born.

Babies born to mothers who used one or more drugs such as heroin, cocaine, PCP, alcohol, and tobacco suffer in a variety of ways and degrees. The amount and the kind of drug use and the health of the mother are just some of the factors that play a part.

No one knows what the future of many of these babies will be, but, five years after the introduction of crack, large numbers of babies who were abused by its use before birth have entered kindergarten. Most schools are not ready for the special needs of these children. In some school districts, teachers are being trained to work with drug-exposed children, but many places do not have the money to provide the kind of care these special children need, care that costs many times more than that for most students.

Many health-care workers point out that drug-exposed newborns, who may tremble and cry twenty-four hours a day, have trouble forming bonds of closeness to other humans. Damage to their nervous systems hinders the development of attachments to parents or others who care for them early in life. Thus they do not learn how to experience love, joy, sadness, guilt, and other emotions the way most people do. Children who cannot love pass on their misery to children of their own. This alone shows that the prevention of abuse is one of the most important problems of our time.

A number of states have added "drug abuse

during pregnancy" to their child abuse laws. The first mother convicted of delivering drugs to her baby through the bloodstream was sentenced to fifteen years of probation and ordered to complete a drug treatment course. By May of 1990 thirty women had been charged as criminals for delivering drugs to a minor when they used drugs during pregnancy. Many others were just referred to treatment programs.

Many people believe that they can help to prevent the birth of drug-exposed babies by punishing the pregnant mothers. Some states have passed laws and convicted pregnant women who use drugs, but there are questions about the value of such laws. Would money be better spent on education and counseling? Will the remote threat of jail keep pregnant women from using drugs? Will pregnant women who use alcohol or smoke cigarettes—legal activities for those over twenty-one—be considered criminals because they harm the children they will bear?

No matter what the law, the harm to babies whose mothers abuse drugs concerns people of all ages, races, and beliefs. Foster-care systems, health-care systems, educators, taxpayers, and families all suffer the consequences.

Specialists in child abuse are taking an increasing interest in encouraging education and support services for pregnant women in the hope that they can help to reduce the abuse of babies before they are born. Many volunteers are giving doses of affection to sick and abandoned babies in some of the hospitals and day-care centers where they live. Many of these children have no place to go, even when they are well enough to leave the hospital. So many infants are deserted by their drug-abusing and AIDS-infected mothers that boarder baby programs have been started in some hospitals. Volunteers come to these hospitals once a week to cuddle the babies and play with them.

As long ago as 1969, Mother Clara Hale began caring for babies born to drug-addicted mothers. What started as a home for a few foster children grew to become Hale House Center in New York City. More than 800 children have been cared for by Hale House, which has expanded to include babies born with AIDS. Most children, who range in age from birth to three years, are referred by police, hospital workers, and social workers, but the first drug-addicted baby was referred to Mother Hale by her daughter, Lorraine, who saw a drugged mother trying to hold onto a baby on a street corner.

The goals at Hale House include the provision of a safe and secure living environment for children and reuniting children with their families after parents have undergone rehabilitation. Babies

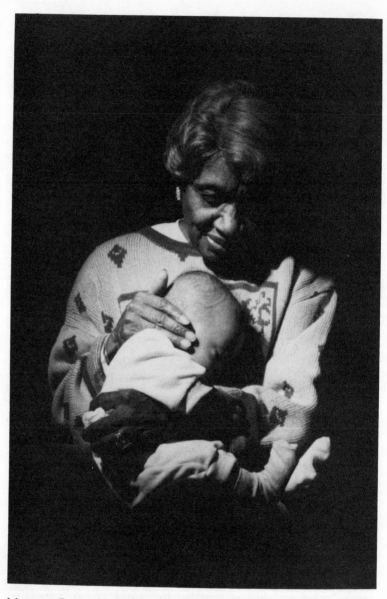

MOTHER CLARA HALE IS FAMOUS FOR HER WORK OF CARING FOR
BABIES OF DRUG-ADDICTED MOTHERS.

are admitted without regard to race, religion, or sex.

Unfortunately, there are far too few programs that help pregnant women and their babies with drug problems. A number of churches, health-care agencies, and recovery centers are trying to help, but this is just a beginning. The fight to save babies and their parents from the effects of crack and other drugs is everyone's fight.

4.

Abused and Homeless

Thousands of children have no real homes. Some of them live with their own families who are homeless. Some of them have run away or have been pushed out of their homes by their families. In every case, these boys and girls suffer from neglect and abuse, some of which is so severe that people find it hard to believe.

Suppose your parents were so poor that you were always hungry unless you found food in trash cans, you slept in the family's van, and you spent your days begging on the street. Or suppose you were homeless and moved every month or so to a different shelter. You had to change schools, had to make new friends wherever you could find them, and had no permanent address for a library card.

Many of the neighborhoods in which homeless children live are full of violence, rats, roaches, and trash. Lack of space in which to play and feel safe is just part of their abuse. Once most of the homeless who lived in parks, on beaches, and in public shelters were adults, but the fastest-growing segment of the homeless population today is families with children.

Eight-year-old Eric was not a homeless kid by choice. He and his mother came to New York to help care for his sick grandmother. After her death, they had to look for another place to live. They could not go back home because they had used all their money.

Two days after his grandmother's funeral, Eric and his mother went to an emergency center, hoping to find a place to stay. The social worker there helped them fill out forms. Then she told Eric's mother to wait for her assignment to a shelter. There were many other people with children in the waiting room. Cribs with dirty sheets held two babies each. Other babies played on the floor or slept in their mothers' arms. Trash was strewn all over the floor. It was so dirty that one mother found a broom and swept some of the dirty papers and cigarette butts into a pile in one corner.

Eric made friends with a boy about his own age. They played together for a while, but an older boy punched them both and took their toys. Eric went back to his mother, curled up in the chair next to her, and finally fell asleep.

About four in the morning, a van took Eric and his mother to a room in an old hotel, where they lived for several months. Most children who lived in the building were afraid to play outside, but they all complained that staying inside was boring. Drug dealers usually hung around outside, selling their crack to people in cars who stopped only long enough to deal, then drove away. Shoot-outs among rival gang members made the streets unsafe. One of Eric's new friends was killed by a stray bullet when she went to the store for a loaf of bread. Eric, his mother, and many of their neighbors lived in a state of fear, day after day.

Eric met a girl who told him about the medical van that used to bring a doctor and nurse to the building to treat the sick people who lived there. The week before, two bullets had been fired into the van while the doctor was examining a child. Although no one was injured, the staff of the health project that provided the van was trying to find a safer place to take care of the children.

When Eric went to school, other children teased him because he lived at a welfare hotel, and he was ashamed to bring classmates home after school. Eric and his mother are just one of hundreds of families who make up the population of the homeless.

Homeless parents who never abused their children before often strike out at them because of the stress of their lives. Many of them suffer from problems that make it impossible to provide the kind of care their children need.

Perhaps there is a homeless boy or girl in your

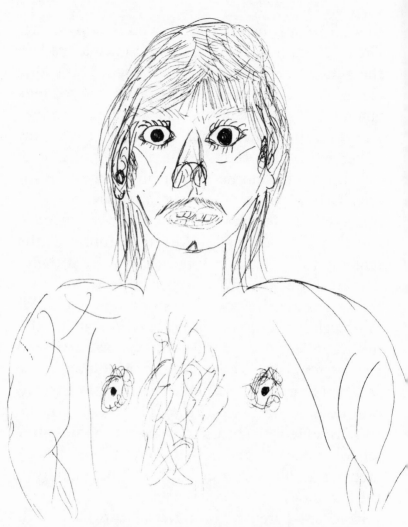

THE CASE HISTORY OF THE ADOLESCENT WHO MADE THIS DRAWING
REVEALS THAT SHE WAS SEXUALLY ABUSED BY HER FATHER, WHO
BLAMES HER FOR THE ABUSE. THE GIRL FIRST RAN AWAY AT AGE
FOUR, AND HAS RUN AWAY 110 TIMES. EXPERTS SAY THERE IS
GENDER CONFUSION IN THE DRAWING, AND THAT AGGRESSION IS
APPARENT IN THE STRONG LINES ABOUT THE FACE AND BODY AND IN
THE PROMINENT TEETH AND EYES.

class. You can help by being friendly and understanding some of the problems that come with being homeless. Even if you never meet a homeless boy or girl, there are many small actions, such as supplying a few cans of food for emergency food kitchens, that can help to prevent abuse among the children who have no real homes.

An estimated one to 2 million boys and girls run away from home and spend a night or two away before they return. However, some teenagers leave their families for good. Runaways appear to be homeless by choice, but 80 percent of them have been so abused that they prefer to struggle with the problems of surviving on the street rather than live at home. Some teens leave because they feel their parents are unreasonable, because they feel unwanted, or for many other reasons. Usually, the act of running away is a cry for help. Many runaways come from homes where parents are separated and a companion or stepparent has entered the family.

No one knows how many boys and girls leave their families and stay away long enough to be counted as homeless each year, but the first federal government effort to count them estimated the number at 500,000. Many people who work with runaways and throwaways, children whose parents don't want them at home, believe this number is far too low. The Department of Health and Human

Services estimates that there may be 2 million. Only about 6,000 beds, nationwide, are available for them each night.

Twelve-year-old Tracy is one of the many young people who leave home because they feel unwanted. She was forced to do chores that were normally done by parents, but her mother and her mother's boyfriend were too busy drinking and having a good time to take care of everyday business, such as cooking, cleaning, earning money, and having fun with the family. One time Tracy overheard the mother's friend saying there must be a way to get rid of "the kid." After that, she was sure things would never get better.

The next night Tracy packed her belongings and took a bus to the nearest city. She became one of the group known as throwaways, thrownaways, or pushouts. Tracy became part of a street family that included others who had left home for similar reasons.

Many throwaways go to the homes of friends or relatives. Others call hotlines, such as those described later in this book, to get help in finding temporary places to live or to get messages home without being hassled.

Mirabel ran away from home when she was eleven years old. Her parents argued all the time, and she felt she had to get out of the house. Mirabel was sure she could get a job in the city as a young model. She looked older than her age, and everyone told her she was beautiful. Her father had already found her attractive sexually, and this was one of the reasons she knew she had to leave. She could not stand his fondling, so she left a note telling her parents not to worry about her. She would find a job in New York.

Mirabel was looking in the phone book for addresses of modeling agencies when a well-dressed man came by and gave her his card. It listed his offices in New York and Beverly Hills. Mirabel was thrilled when he suggested she come to his office for test photos. He explained that his secretary would be there to help her with her makeup, and she would be allowed a half hour for her first photos. This seemed like a great opportunity. She felt very lucky to have been invited to try out for a job at a large agency where there would be a secretary to make her feel safe.

When Mirabel reached the address on the card, she was surprised to find the building less attractive than she had expected it to be. However, she was eager for a job, so she went inside. When the photographer answered the door, Mirabel asked about his secretary. He explained that she had taken some film to the developers.

The first photo was taken of Mirabel's face. The photographer then explained that he wanted her to model some bathing suits. Mirabel felt uncomfortable about this, but she knew that her clothing was not suitable for ads. Maybe she was just overly suspicious. Before she had time to put on the first bathing suit, the photographer told her he needed a few pictures of her without clothing. Mirabel refused to pose this way, but the man was stronger than she was. When she tried to leave, he grabbed her by the hair and screamed at her. She was his prisoner for six hours. When he fell into a drunken sleep on the couch, Mirabel managed to get some of her clothes on and run out of the building.

Within a week, Mirabel learned that the only way she could survive in New York was to join a street family of girls who sold their bodies for sexual favors. She still hoped that someday she would get a modeling job, but she was beginning to hate herself. She did not eat or sleep well, and her skin was covered with pimples. Life was terrible in New York. Finally she called her mother's cousin and went to live with her. She found a job in a supermarket, where she made enough money to help pay for her board. She gave up hope of becoming a model, but she felt safe. Someday she would go to school and find a better job.

Not all runaways are as lucky as Mirabel. As many as 200 unidentified children are found dead each year. Boys and girls who manage to call families or hotlines suffer less abuse than those who remain on the street. The National Network of Runaway and Youth Services runs about 500 shelters around the nation, but they have to turn away as many as 3,000 young people each year for lack of space. Hotline workers help their callers find food, temporary places to live, and counselors to talk with them about their problems.

Although many adults believe that all runaways are "bad kids" who run away to upset their parents, most of these young people are fleeing bad situations at home. There is no typical runaway or homeless youth, but most of them are between the ages of twelve and eighteen. They belong to every race and come from poor, middle-class, and wealthy families. They come from every neighborhood and state in the nation. Most teens who live in street families become involved in petty theft, drug dealing, prostitution, and/or child pornography in order to survive.

Both homeless children who live with families and those who run away from their families suffer a great deal of abuse. Help is available from sources listed at the back of this book.

5.

Children of Battered Women

Studies show that about one in every ten women is abused every year by the man with whom they live. Three to 4 million women in the United States live with this kind of violence. Many thousands of children grow up in families in which their fathers control behavior by physical force. In a small percentage of cases, women batter the man of the house.

No one knows how many children witness violence in their homes, but some children tell heartbreaking stories at shelters for battered women. In one case, a father dragged his children from their beds in the middle of the night and made them sit along the side of the room while he hit their mother with a baseball bat. He was angry because she did not have dinner ready when he came home from work.

While some children witness the violence directly, some hear it from a different room. In many cases, these boys and girls blame themselves for the battering, even though they are not sure what they might have done to cause it. Now and then,

SHELTERS LET FAMILIES RETURN TO A MORE NORMAL ROUTINE, AND
EVEN ALLOW FOR SOME FUN. IN THE TOP PHOTO, A FAMILY TAKES A
MOMENT TO HAVE THEIR PICTURE TAKEN DURING THE SON'S THIRD
BIRTHDAY PARTY, HELD AT THE SHELTER DURING THE FAMILY'S
THREE-MONTH STAY. THE MOTHER AND DAUGHTER IN THE BOTTOM
PHOTO HAD THEIR FACES PAINTED AT A VALENTINE'S DAY PARTY
COSPONSORED BY THE DOMESTIC VIOLENCE SHELTER WHERE THEY
RESIDED.

a child strikes out with a knife or a gun at a father or other man who is hurting his or her mother. Some of these children are as young as three.

Tod grew up in a family where wife beating was common. His mother was one of many women whose husbands feel that they can, and should, control their women by violence. Tod, who often watched his father beat his mother, learned that violence is the way to get people to do what you want them to do. Tod was known at school as a bully; he made friends with smaller children and forced them to do what he wanted by fighting.

When the principal called Tod to his office and pointed out the many reports he had of Tod's roughness to younger children, Tod explained that kids were always picking on him. His father had told him that he must always be in control. Tod believed he had to be tough so no "little mama's boy" would put anything over on him. He blamed others for the fights. He did not realize that he was the one who stirred up trouble.

When the schoolyard fights continued and Tod was especially rough on a younger boy, the principal asked the school counselor to help. She insisted that Tod's parents come to school to discuss his behavior. His mother had a black eye, so his father went alone.

At the meeting, Tod's father offered to punish him for any bad behavior at school. He told the counselor that he could control his family. Tod's father explained that Tod had been cured of his stubbornness because he had beaten the badness out of Tod when he was little. The counselor realized that telling his father about the schoolyard fights would mean beatings for Tod, so she asked for permission to work with Tod. When his father was told that this would keep Tod from being expelled, he consented.

The counselor soon discovered that Tod was a very frightened boy. He picked on smaller kids because he felt helpless and overwhelmed by the need to behave well at home. Tod was afraid of his father, whose beatings of Tod had been cruel. He was especially upset when his father beat his mother, because Tod felt he should do something to protect her.

After many sessions with the counselor at school, Tod began to trust adult men and realize that not all men rule by force. His counselor was able to give Tod a different view of the world around him and showed him how to live without the need for violence.

Controlling others by power and force is something many men learn as they are growing up. The women they live with often have been brought up believing that they should be submissive to their partners. This sets the stage for battering and for suffering by the children of battered women.

Battering tends to go through several stages. There is a stage in which there are small arguments and small hurts. This kind of behavior lasts for about a month. Then the batterer reaches the explosive stage and beats his partner severely. After this he is sorry and may bring gifts along with promises to change. But the cycle of abuse continues. In addition to concern for their own safety, these women never know when their children will be hurt physically or made to witness violence against their mothers.

Batterers tend to keep their families away from other people in order to decrease the chances of exposure. Even when injured women and children come in contact with others, they are secretive about their injuries. Black eyes, cuts, and bruises are explained with lies to protect the abuser. Fear of more violence prevents many battered women and their children from telling anyone what is happening at home.

Why would a mother protect the man who hurt her by making up stories to explain her injuries? Why do battered women stay with these men? The answers to these questions are many, and the reasons are complicated. Each case is different, but there are some common threads.

Often battered women have been made to feel worthless by their partners. They begin to believe they are so worthless that they deserve the abuse.

Another reason for putting up with the violence at home is simply not having anyplace else to go. Although these women never know when they will be tied to the bed, beaten, or even killed, they may tolerate the violence for years.

Some women manage to escape from the abuse by fleeing to a shelter for battered women and their children. Many secretly pack clothes, sleepwear, medicine, toilet articles, and money, and leave in the night with their children. They manage to get to a shelter whose address they have learned of through a hotline or a community service. The addresses of such shelters are kept secret from men so that batterers cannot follow.

At the shelter, a counselor and other women who have been battered make the newcomers feel welcome. They help them to get temporary restraining orders, which are papers from a judge that tell the abusers to stay away from the families they have been hurting. Some men are ordered to get out of the house. Later, women fill out forms telling the details of what has been happening to them and why they need help for themselves and their children.

Sometimes abusers do not obey the orders, and further tragedies occur. There have been cases where battered women have killed their partners in order to protect themselves and their children. Many communities are working to help families before such extreme actions take place.

In many cases, women do not report what has happened to them because they fear this will make things worse. Sometimes it does, but new laws in a number of states are making it possible for police to arrest a man who has been reported on the chance that he will hurt a woman. New guidelines are sending a stronger message that domestic violence is a crime.

Support groups for battered women and their children are spreading, but much remains to be done. More shelters for battered women are needed desperately. Education about how these women can break away from the hurt, as well as more help for their children, can improve all their futures. Although some programs exist that teach men ways of handling problems without violence, there are not enough of them. Some partner battering happens only when the abusers have been drinking or using other drugs. More drug prevention and treatment programs can help to prevent abuse too.

Battering is not an illness, it is learned behavior. Abuse of female partners is a major social and criminal problem in our society, and the children of battered women and abusive men are affected directly and indirectly. This is true whether or not the batterer is the father of the child.

Battering women is not a private matter. Its effects extend far beyond the closed doors behind which it occurs.

6.

Sexual Abuse

*E*xperts estimate that one in three girls and one in eight boys under the age of eighteen will be involved in some form of forced sexual experience. After Maxie's mother and father read this, they were very careful to make her understand that she had the right to say no if someone wanted to touch her in a way that made her feel uncomfortable. This included people she knew and loved.

Maxie's parents told her again and again to be careful about strangers who might try to be friendly. They made so much fuss about what might happen to her that she was afraid to answer anyone she did not know. For instance, when a new neighbor asked her if she liked school, Maxie turned her head away and pretended that she did not hear him. Maxie thought anyone she did not know might kidnap her and do awful things to her. She lived in a world of fear.

Maxie was afraid of touches, too. She jumped away when her teacher patted her on the shoulder. He just wanted to comfort her after she finished reading a story about how her cat died. Maxie

65

HUGS ARE A GOOD FORM OF TOUCHING.

missed many other good touches, too, because her parents had frightened her so. Maxie's parents did not mean to scare her about strangers or about the good kinds of touches. They just wanted to be sure that she was safe.

When Emily's mother and father talked to her about strangers and about touching, they were careful to explain the difference between safe and unsafe conversations and about good touches and bad touches. They told her that most people are good, but there are some strangers who lure children with candy, requests for help, and other tricks in order to get the children to go with them. Then they sexually abuse the boys and girls and they may keep them from returning to their parents. In rare cases, they even kill them. This is one reason that people become so upset when a child is missing.

You may have seen pictures of missing children on milk cartons and on posters in your neighborhood. Most missing children have been taken by a parent who has been refused custody, or care, of them after a divorce. These children may be hidden by the parents who steal them, may move frequently, change their names, and be kept from using the telephone to call home to the parents from whom they have been taken. Although they are abused because of the conditions in which they must live, their abuse is usually only emotional. The boys and girls who are stolen by strangers often suffer sexual abuse.

Most sexual abuse of children involves someone other than a stranger. That is why Emily's parents were so careful to explain to her the difference between good and bad touching. Hugs are a wonderful part of life. Snuggling in bed with a parent on a cold night or holding a new baby brother or sister can feel wonderful. Handshakes, holding hands, and kissing someone you love are good touches. Tickling can feel good if the tickler stops when asked.

Emily did not like it when her neighbor tickled her because he touched her in places that made her feel uncomfortable. She told him to stop, and when he refused, she left the room. Her sister thought this was rude, but their mother said Emily was right in behaving the way she did.

Every child has the right to say no to any touch that involves sexual parts or is scary or uncomfortable. You can say, "That part of my body is private. Don't touch me there." Or you can refuse to touch someone anyplace, or in any way, that makes you feel uncomfortable. It is good to tell an adult you can trust if someone touches your breasts, penis, or any sexual part. This kind of secret should be told.

Ten-year-old Kevin and his mother never talked about good and bad touches. Kevin lived alone with his mother for three years, and he missed his father, who moved over a hundred miles away. Their neighbor, Marvin, took him on fishing trips, camping trips, and taught him to play tennis. All of this attention pleased Kevin's mother, who worried about how much he missed his father.

Although most men who are good companions to young boys have no plans to molest them sexually, Marvin was setting up a special relationship so that he could persuade Kevin to provide sexual favors. When he asked Kevin to undress and sit on his lap, he told him that this would be their special secret. He was never to tell anyone.

Kevin found sexual touching scary, and after a

number of secret events, he told his mother. She scolded him for making up such a story about a man who had been so nice to him.

Kevin was very upset when his mother did not believe him, and he felt he must tell someone. His teacher was more understanding. When Kevin told her the secret, she asked him if she might share it with the school nurse, Ms. Goodrich. Since Ms. Goodrich had been trained to talk with children about abuse problems, she spent long hours with Kevin, helping him to understand that what had happened was not his fault. She gave him courage to tell Marvin that he did not want to be the kind of friend he was looking for, and she assured Kevin that she would be there to help if he had another problem. Kevin's mother took part in some of the conversations with the nurse. After this, his mother was more understanding and more ready to listen to Kevin's problems.

Many boys and girls who are sexually abused do not get help. They suffer for many years, and in some cases, they abuse their own children. Many victims suffer from emotional problems all their lives. They feel fear, shame, and guilt even though the abuse was not their fault. Fortunately, there are many hotlines and places where children and where adults who were molested as children can get help. Some of these are listed at the end of this book.

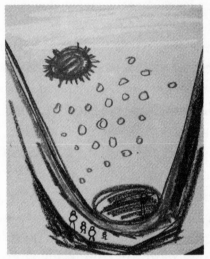

THESE DRAWINGS BY SEXUALLY ABUSED CHILDREN EXPRESS THE
FEELING OF BEING TRAPPED IN A HORRIBLE SITUATION. IN THE UPPER
DRAWING, THE CHILD IS SURROUNDED BY TEETH. IN THE BOTTOM
DRAWING, THE FIGURES AT THE LEFT REPRESENT THE OTHER
MEMBERS OF THE FAMILY, WHO ARE OUTSIDE THE "HOT CIRCLE" OF
ABUSE.

70

One of the most upsetting kinds of sexual abuse, and one of the most common, is incest. Incest is the term used for sexual abuse by a close relative. Boys and girls whose parents sexually abuse them have an especially difficult problem. They are hurt by someone they have learned to trust. Many times, when they find the courage to tell the parent who is not involved, they are not believed.

Through the ages, most of these "secrets" were kept for a whole lifetime. Adults who were molested as children continued to feel shame, guilt, and suffer from deeply rooted emotional stress. Today, there are many kinds of help available for victims of incest. Groups of adults who were molested as children meet and talk about their feelings. Sometimes, the memory of the abuse is buried so deeply that it does not come to mind until a therapist helps a person with other problems, many of which actually resulted from the incest.

Survivors of sexual abuse suffer many kinds of long-term effects, such as difficulty trusting others, being loving and caring parents and spouses, having eating disorders, nightmares, and other problems. Some learn to forgive, but others carry the scars throughout their lives.

In addition to actual physical contact, sexual abuse takes a number of forms. It may involve children in pictures of nude adults or taking pictures of children without clothing and in positions that excite viewers. Many pictures are sold to black-market magazines.

Knowing about sexual abuse can help you to prevent it from happening to you. Know that sexual abuse can develop slowly over a long period of time, that it can be committed by people of every religious background, race, and income. Many sexual abusers of young children are teenage boys.

Most often, the abuser is someone the young person knows, such as a brother or sister or other member of a family, a baby-sitter, a friend, or leader of a group to which they belong. This does not mean that one should be afraid of being abused by Boy Scout leaders and other group leaders. Only a very small percentage of these people are child abusers.

The important thing in preventing sexual abuse is to know that your body is your own and you have the right to say no. And if you have been abused, know that sexual abuse by an adult is never your fault. You have a right to seek help.

7.

What Can You Do?

Abuse does not have to happen. When it does, there are many ways to reach out for help. Unfortunately, many victims do not know how.

Suppose your friend Marnie confides in you that her father is molesting her. She does not want to upset her mother, who has been sick for a long time. Her mother probably would not believe her anyhow. Marnie has told her father to stop, but he tells her that they are just expressing their love for each other the way many fathers and daughters do. Marnie knows that he is wrong, but she loves her father, and she is afraid that he will go to jail if she tells the police.

Sometimes Marnie feels that some of the problem is her own fault. Would she be sent to foster care if she told? You can see that Marnie is very upset, and you really want to help your friend. But what can you do? She just wants to talk to you about her secret; she does not want you to do anything about it.

Although you know Marnie needs to tell an adult, you must be careful not to ask her about details just to satisfy your own curiosity. You have already helped Marnie by listening to her as a friend. You must let her know that you care about her and that you still like her. You can promise her you will not tell everybody. But should you tell someone?

First, you can try to persuade Marnie to tell an adult she can trust. You can suggest ways of telling someone, and she could practice what she might say to that person by saying it to you. Offer to go with her to see a counselor if this will make it easier for her.

Marnie may feel more comfortable telling her secret to someone she does not know, such as a hotline crisis worker or a counselor at the local mental-health center, if there is one in her area. Suggest hotline numbers listed at the back of this book.

However, if you find that Marnie is not going to tell an adult who can help her, or if she tries to get help and cannot, you should go to an adult you can trust for help. Although Marnie made you promise you would not tell her secret, this is the kind of secret that should be told in order for someone to help. This does not mean you should gossip with friends about it. You could talk to a teacher, a school counselor, one of your parents, your minister, rabbi, or priest, your doctor, another relative, or any other adult you like and feel you can trust. This person may be able to tell you what kind of help is available in your neighborhood or find out what Marnie should do.

Talking about abuse is scary because it is such a serious problem. Many young people think that telling will mean that the abuser will be sent to jail. This probably will not happen, but, in the case of sexual abuse, the offender may have to move out of the home until his or her treatment program has been completed. Social workers will probably work with the whole family. In some areas, social workers are being assigned to spend several hours a day, several days a week for a month with a troubled family in an effort to prevent abuse and preserve the family as a unit.

Child abusers are not cruel people who want to hurt their children. They simply do not know how to be good parents. Some parents abuse their children because they believe this is the way they should be disciplined. They never learned the right ways to discipline their children or how to cope with stress. However, many parents who were mistreated as they were growing up do not abuse their children.

Juan's mother thought she could teach him not to play with matches by burning him with a cigarette. She made one burn on his arm the first time she saw him trying to light a cigarette the way she did. The next time she burned him in three places.

Juan's mother grew up in a family that used violence to control children. She suffered severe punishments rather than quiet discipline, such as "time out" sitting in a chair for a while. She abused her child the way her parents abused her, until she got help from Parents Anonymous (PA). This organization has chapters nationwide. Groups of parents who have abused their children, or fear that they might, join to express their problems and learn better ways of parenting. There are no fees, and no one is required to reveal his or her name. A person who runs the meetings is trained to help the parents, but in many cases they help one another. Telephone numbers are exchanged and used when there is a crisis. A fellow member may remind the person who calls of some of the suggested alternatives to lashing out at a child. Counting to ten or twenty, pressing lips together and breathing deeply, saying the alphabet, taking a hot bath or splashing cold water on one's face, writing one's thoughts on paper, hugging a pillow, closing one's eyes and imagining what a child is hearing are some of the ways that help to prevent a parent from abusing a child.

If you know a family in which abuse is taking place, you might make them aware of the PA phone number. Posting information, including the local phone number that can be found in your phone book, in a place this family frequents may be a way to help. Or, if you have a friend who is suffering abuse, the friend may be able to persuade his or her parents to call a hotline number so that a counselor can suggest how to get help.

You can ask your teacher to include the subject of child abuse in your social studies program. There is a great deal of literature available from the organizations listed at the end of this book. You might study about someone like Francine.

Francine's mother never meant to hurt her. She, like many other abusive parents, lived alone and was overworked. When the stress built up, she lashed out at Francine. One time she cut her daughter with a knife because she would not clean up the mess she made in the kitchen. Francine's mother was sorry after it happened, and she promised not to do anything like that again. However, each time Francine's disobedience added stress to her mother's already difficult life, she beat her or abused her in some other physical way.

Francine learned to stay away from home when her mother had a bad day. When she didn't get out of the way, she covered her bruises with long sleeves or excuses. Francine thought she was helping her mother by not telling anyone. If there is someone you know who thinks she or he must tolerate being abused, that person can learn how to reach out for help.

If you feel that you need to talk to someone

about yourself, you should know that you can stop the abuse and get help for everyone in your family. Child abuse is against the law. Every state has laws to protect children and help to make their homes safe.

Some communities have special services to help. If you cannot find help locally through a trusted adult or a local hotline, there are nationwide hotlines to call.

When a hotline is reached, a trained worker talks to the caller to see if the report seems true, makes sure children in the family are safe, and offers help. You do not have to give a name in order to get help. The hotline worker may suggest ways a parent can get help with a drug problem, with finances, with parenting skills, or can get counseling. Or, if the caller is not safe in his or her home, instructions for reaching a safe place will be provided.

If parents refuse to stop hurting a child and will not cooperate by going to programs that will help, they may have to go to a family court. In the case of sexual abuse or severe physical abuse, parents may have to go to a criminal court. The purpose of this court is protection of the family, not punishment.

If you report abuse, whether it involves you or someone else, you will need to talk about what has been happening so that a social worker can help.

It is important to tell the truth. Child abuse reports are very serious; they are not a way to get back at parents, teachers, or someone you do not like. They should not be used in an effort to get parents to be less strict, to get out of the house because you hate the rules they make, or to manipulate something, or someone, to your advantage.

If you have a question about whether or not you are really being abused, it is important to tell someone. If you are being abused sexually, or being severely hurt or neglected, continue to tell someone until you are believed and until you get help. This may take a lot of courage, but you have a right to a life in which you are not being hurt all the time.

If you suspect child abuse, or need to talk to someone yourself, you can call 1-800-4-A-CHILD (1-800-422-4453). This is the nation's largest child abuse hotline. In addition to phone counseling, this hotline provides information on reporting and preventing child abuse.

Another hotline number for abused children and adults is 1-800-333-SAFE (7233). This hotline is open twenty-four hours a day and will provide information about where you can get help locally.

Where to Find Help

National Hotlines

Boys Town: 1-800-448-3000

Childhelp USA: 1-800-4-A-CHILD (1-800-422-4453)

Domestic Violence Hotline: 1-800-333-SAFE (7233)

National Center for Missing and Exploited Children: 1-800-843-5678

National Directory of Children, Youth, and Families Services: 1-800-343-6681

National Runaway Switchboard: 1-800-621-4000

Nineline: 1-800-999-9999

Parents Anonymous: 1-800-421-0353
In California: 1-800-352-0386

Runaway Hotline: 1-800-231-6946
In Texas: 1-800-392-3352

Sources of Information and Community Services

Adolescent Abuse
Communications and Public Service
Boys Town, Nebraska 68010

Clearinghouse on Child Abuse and Neglect Information
P.O. Box 1182
Washington, D.C. 20013

National Committee for the Prevention of Child Abuse
322 South Michigan Avenue, Suite 1250
Chicago, Illinois 60604

Look in your phone book for local community services.

Glossary

Abandonment. leaving children without caregivers. In medieval times, it was not uncommon for immature parents to abandon a child to a wet nurse, foster family, monastery, nunnery, or servants.

Addict. a person who depends on a drug for normal functioning.

Battered child syndrome. children whose injuries are said to have come from accidental causes but are the result of intentional physical damage. A term coined by Henry Kempe and his colleagues in 1962.

Boarder babies. babies and toddlers who remain in the hospital after they are well enough to leave because there is no place for them to go.

Cold turkey. an abrupt discontinuation of drug use. Withdrawal symptoms that result depend on the kind and amount of the drug as well as other factors, such as the general health of the individual.

Crack. a smokable form of cocaine that is highly addictive and relatively inexpensive.

Emotional abuse. a way of affecting feelings of a person through a variety of ways, such as humiliation, social isolation, constant rejection, and use of negative criticism.

Some parents use children to satisfy their own needs for approval, rather than being supportive.

Fetal alcohol syndrome (FAS). a condition resulting from alcohol use by a mother during pregnancy. Children may be affected in varying degrees. Symptoms may include brain damage, abnormal facial development, problems with hearing and vision, and other problems.

Fetus. a developed embryo in the womb; a human embryo more than eight weeks after conception.

Hepatitis. a disease that can be transferred from person to person through dirty needles used in intravenous drug abuse. There are many other ways of spreading this disease that affects the liver.

Heroin. a powerful sedative drug made from morphine, used chiefly by addicts.

Incest. sexual abuse by a family member.

LSD (lysergic acid diethylamide). a powerful drug that produces hallucinations, the illusion of seeing or hearing something that is not present.

Marijuana. dried leaves, stems, and flowering tops of the hemp plant, usually smoked in cigarette form.

Methadone. an addictive drug used in treatment programs to wean addicts from heroin.

PCP (phencyclidine). highly addictive drug that causes hallucinations and frequently causes aggressive, uncontrollable behavior. Commonly called angel dust.

Penis. male sex organ.

Placenta. an organ that develops in the womb during pregnancy and supplies the fetus with nourishment.

Street drugs. illegal drugs of unknown strength sold by dealers who may themselves be addicts. Many street drugs contain impurities.

Sudden infant death syndrome (SID). crib death, a condition in which apparently healthy babies die suddenly in their sleep.

Uterus. a hollow organ in which a baby is conceived and nourished before birth; womb.

For Further Reading

Check, William A. *Child Abuse*. New York: Chelsea House, 1990.

Cooney, Judith. *Coping with Child Abuse*. New York: Rosen Publishing Group, 1987.

Fontana, Vincent. *Somewhere A Child is Crying*. New York: NAL-Dutton, 1989.

Hyde, Margaret O. *Cry Softly: The Story of Child Abuse*. Louisville, KY: Westminster/John Knox Press. 1986.

Hyde, Margaret O. *Sexual Abuse: Let's Talk About It*. Louisville, KY: Westminster/John Knox, 1984.

Hyde, Margaret O., and Elizabeth Forsyth. *The Violent Mind*. New York: Franklin Watts, 1991.

Landau, Elaine. *Child Abuse: An American Epidemic*. New York: Messner, 1990.

Mufson, Susan, and Rachel Kranz. *Straight Talk About Child Abuse*. New York: Facts on File, 1991.

Stewart, Gail. *Child Abuse*. New York: Macmillan, 1989.

Index

Abandonment, 6, 37
Adolescents:
  abuse of, 18–19, 21–22
  coping by abused, 18–19
  pregnant, *see* Pregnant
    women, drug abusing
  runaways, 47–51
  throwaways, 47–51
  troublemaking by abused,
    20–21
Age of abused, 15–23
Aggressive behavior, child's,
    57–58
AIDS, 28, 37
Alcohol abuse, 22
  effect on unborn of, 29–32,
    34–35
American Lung Association,
    29

Babies:
  of drug-using parent, *see*
    Pregnant women, drug
    abusing
  neglect of, 4–6
  physical abuse of, 15–16, 18
Battered child syndrome, 8–9
Battered women. *See* Women,
  battered

Because I Love My Baby, 29
Broken Cord, The (Dorris), 31–
    32
Burns, 4–6, 15–16, 77–78

Child abuse:
  average age, 18
  emotional, *see* Emotional
    abuse
  forms of, 3–4, 9–10
  historically, 6–9
  homeless and, *see* Homeless
    children
  laws, 82
  legal defense of abused chil-
    dren, 8
  parents repeating abuse of
    their childhood, 77–78
  physical, *see* Physical abuse
  psychological, *see* Emo-
    tional abuse
  reporting, 68–69, 76–77,
    82–83
  sexual, *see* Sexual abuse
  statistics on, 9, 10, 11, 21–
    22
  understanding, 4–6, 77
Childhelp USA, 10
Child pornography, 51, 71–72

Cocaine, 28, 34–35
Cold turkey, 28
Community services, 83–84
Crack, 28, 33–35
Crib death, 29

Day-care centers, abuse in, 16–18
Department of Health and Human Services, U.S., 47–48
Domestic Violence. *See* Physical abuse; Women, battered
Dorris, Michael, 31–32
Drug abuse, 19, 22
    effects on babies of parent's abuse, *see* Pregnant women, drug abusing
Drug dealing, 51

Education programs:
    for battered women, 61
    on child abuse, 81
    for pregnant women, 36–37
Elder abuse, 22
Emotional abuse:
    overly protective parent, 11
    verbal battering, 10–11

Fetal alcohol effect (FAE), 31, 32
Fetal alcohol syndrome (FAS), 29–32

Hale, Mother Clara, 37, 38
Hale House Center, 37–39

Helping the abused, 75–81
    finding an adult who can help, 76–77
    getting them to seek help, 75–76
    hotlines, *see* Hotlines
    reporting abuse, 66–69, 76–77, 80–81
Hepatitis B, 28
Heroin, 28, 34–35
Homeless children, 43–51
    helping, 45–47
    peers and, 45
    runaways, 47–51
    shelters, 44–45, 51
    throwaways, 47–51
Hotlines:
    for child abuse, 78–79, 80, 81, 83
    for runaways, 51
    for sexual abuse, 69, 76

Incest, 71–72, 77

Kempe, Dr. C. Henry, 8–9

LSD, 28

Marijuana, 28, 32–33
Methadone, 28
Missing children, 66–67

National Network of Runaway and Youth Services, 50–51
Neglect, case of, 4–6
Nursery schools, abuse in, 16–18

Overly protective parents, 11

Parents Anonymous (PA), 78
PCP, 28, 34–35
Physical abuse, 4, 81
  of babies, 15–16, 18
  as "discipline," 16, 77–78
  hiding, 81
  historically, 6–9
Pregnant women, drug abusing, 27–39
  AIDS and, 28
  alcohol, 29–32
  doctor's care for, 28
  drugs harming unborns, 28
  education and support for, 36–37
  as form of child abuse, 35–36
  smoking, 29
  withdrawal, 28
  see also individual drugs
Prostitution, 50, 51
Psychological abuse. See Emotional abuse

Reporting abuse, 68–71, 76–77, 80–81
Runaways, 47–51

Self-esteem, 19, 20, 59
Sexual abuse, 4, 65–72, 75–77, 80
  counseling, 69, 71, 77
  in day-care situations, 16–18
  fear of, 65–66
  hotlines, 69, 76
  incest, 71–72, 75

long-term effects of, 71
of missing children, 66–67
statistics on, 11
talking to children about, 65–68
telling a trusted adult about, 68–69, 76–77, 81
Shelters:
  domestic violence, 56, 60, 61
  for homeless, 44–45, 51
Smoking, 29
Social workers, 79, 80
Society for the Prevention of Cruelty to Animals, 8
Sudden infant death syndrome, 29
Support groups:
  for battered women, 61
  for child abuse, 78

Teenage mothers, 4–6
  see also Pregnant women, drug abusing
Throwaways, 47–51
Tobacco, 28

Wife beating. See Women, battered
Withdrawal from drugs, 28
Withdrawn behavior, 19
Women, battered:
  children of, 55–61
  the law and, 61
  reasons women stay, 59–60
  shelters for, 56, 60, 61
  stages of battering, 59
  statistics on, 22, 55
  support groups for, 61

93